GET TO WORK!

COOKING GREAT CUISINE WITH A

CHEF

 Gareth Stevens
PUBLISHING

BY JOAN STOLTMAN

Please visit our website, www.garethstevens.com. For a free color catalog of all our high-quality books, call toll free 1-800-542-2595 or fax 1-877-542-2596.

Cataloging-in-Publication Data

Names: Stoltman, Joan.
Title: Cooking great cuisine with a chef / Joan Stoltman.
Description: New York : Gareth Stevens Publishing, 2019. | Series: Get to work! | Includes index.
Identifiers: ISBN 9781538212226 (pbk.) | ISBN 9781538212240 (library bound) | ISBN 9781538212233 (6 pack)
Subjects: LCSH: Cooks–Vocational guidance–Juvenile literature. | Cooking–Vocational guidance–Juvenile literature.
Classification: LCC TX652.5 S7585 2019 | DDC 641.5092–dc23

Published in 2019 by
Gareth Stevens Publishing
111 East 14th Street, Suite 349
New York, NY 10003

Copyright © 2019 Gareth Stevens Publishing

Designer: Bethany Perl
Editor: Joan Stoltman

Photo credits: Cover, p. 1 (chef) Tong_stocker/Shutterstock.com; pp. 1-24 (utensils) TakeStockPhotography/Shutterstock.com; pp. 1-24 (background) MaLija/Shutterstock.com; pp. 1-24 (rectangular banner) punsayaporn/Shutterstock.com; p. 5 Maskot/Getty Images; p. 7 (paperwork) XiXinXing/Shutterstock.com; p. 7 (plating) Africa Studio/Shutterstock.com; pp. 8-18 (text box) LoveVectorGirl/Shutterstock.com; p. 9 (sushi) 135pixels/Shutterstock.com; p. 9 (butcher) PHILIPIMAGE/Shutterstock.com; p. 11 Iakov Filimonov/Shutterstock.com; p. 13 Cultura RM Exclusive/Leon Harris/Cultura Exclusive/Getty Images; p. 15 Hero Images/Stone/Getty Images; pp. 17, 19 (all) wavebreakmedia/Shutterstock.com; p. 21 (breadsticks) JoannaTkaczuk/Shutterstock.com; p. 21 (torn paper and tape) Flas100/Shutterstock.com; p. 21 (stainless steel) most popular/Shutterstock.com.

Printed in the United States of America

CPSIA compliance information: Batch #CS18GS: For further information contact Gareth Stevens, New York, New York at 1-800-542-2595.

CONTENTS

Words in the glossary appear in **bold** type the first time they are used in the text.

CHEF OR COOK?

Some people think chefs and cooks are the same thing, but they aren't. A cook knows how to make food, but a chef is a food artist!

A chef is also in charge of at least part of a kitchen—and sometimes the whole kitchen and **menu**! Kitchens are hot, loud, small, sweaty, and crowded. You have to work quickly, sometimes even running, to make every dish perfect. If that sounds exciting and not scary, being a chef is just the job for you!

Chefs are in charge of **managing** costs and **staff**, ordering supplies, and teaching staff how to create new dishes.

5

WHAT'LL MY JOB BE?

Some kitchens break up work by what the food is. The fish station chef does everything for fish dishes, including buying, preparing, cooking, and plating the fish, which means making it look good on a dish. Other kitchens break up the work by how the food is cooked. Once chef cooks on the grill, another at the fryer, and another at the stove.

You can choose to **specialize** in bread, sauces, or a **cuisine** like Italian, Thai, or even Italian-Thai **fusion**! You can train in sushi, cheese, or ice carving. The choices are truly endless!

Some chefs even own their own **restaurant**, running a kitchen and a business at once!

PLATING

PLACES TO WORK

Hospitals, ships, hotels, schools, event spaces, airports, and so many more kinds of businesses have chefs on staff. Wherever you work, you'll always be part of a team and expected to work hard, listen, and improve.

There are more chef jobs than you can imagine! Chefs **butcher** meat at restaurants. Chefs invent meals for food companies. Chefs remove the bones from fish for **caterers**. Chefs grill at country clubs.

SPEAKING TO THE CHEF

The next time you're out eating, ask to speak to the chef if they have a few minutes. Ask questions about when they became a chef. Don't take up too much of their time!

All kitchens have one thing in common: chefs hard at work!

SUSHI

BEING A HEAD CHEF

A head chef is in charge of a whole kitchen. As head chef, you'll invent your own dishes! More than just making up a **recipe**, you'll also have to figure out what the **ingredients** cost and how long it takes to make. These numbers help you decide what price to sell it for.

You'll also need to decide what staff will prepare it, how you'll plate it, and how you'll write it up on the menu.

BE A SOUS CHEF!

A sous (SOO) chef is the main helper to a head chef. Imagine your home kitchen is a fancy restaurant, and practice being the sous chef for the day!

A kitchen staff is a team. They must be able to talk and listen to each other. Everyone must trust and help each other.

11

HOW DO I BECOME A CHEF?

Some people go to culinary, or cooking, school to learn how to be a chef. There are 1-year, 2-year, and 4-year school tracks. At the very least, you'll learn basic kitchen skills, like how to cut quickly or decorate baked goods. The more years in culinary school, the more skills you'll learn.

At a culinary school, you'll have the opportunity to try out many stations and ways of cooking to find what you're good at and what you love.

PRACTICE YOUR TOSS!

Have a family member prepare several salad ingredients for you. Practice mixing, or tossing, it all together. Don't forget to toss in the dressing!

You need to be on time, dress well, work hard, and be ready to learn at culinary school. If you do this, the teachers may help find you a job when you finish school!

CULINARY SCHOOL

It can cost a lot of money to go to a good culinary school. However, you'll never be surrounded by more chefs. You can learn something from each chef you meet! When it comes to food, you can never know everything. There are always new dishes, **flavors**, tricks, and recipes to learn.

If you want to own a restaurant one day, you can take business and management classes, too. You can also go to school later in life if you're not ready to own a business right away.

You may want to spend time in a busy kitchen before you apply to culinary school. Make sure you want to be a chef!

15

STARTING YOUR CAREER

Even after culinary school, you may have to start at the bottom and work your way up. That often means working as a dishwasher or preparing food for the other chefs. You'll still get to know everyone in the kitchen. When a job opens up, owners often hire the people already working there!

Because of this and cost, many chefs don't go to culinary school. They go straight to work. In fact, many successful chefs on TV didn't learn their skills at school!

DO YOUR VEGGIE HOMEWORK

Ride along on your family's next food-shopping trip with some paper and a pencil. Write down the names of vegetables you've never tried, then look them up when you get home!

There's so much to learn from working in a kitchen. Going straight to work is often a great way to train, make money, and learn real-life skills.

TRAINING FOREVER?!

Being a chef means always learning. Chefs read cookbooks, travel books, restaurant reviews, food websites, recipes, and cooking magazines. Chefs even study other chefs' menus! Chefs travel to learn new cuisines or different takes on dishes, seeing how other people live, eat, and cook. Chefs don't just eat a new ingredient and say "yum!" They go home and try to cook with that new ingredient!

The more you practice, the better you'll be. Every kitchen skill—from cutting and pouring to butchering and baking—can be done faster, cleaner, better, or all three!

TIME TO TASTE TEST

Line up the spice jars from your home on a table. Pour out a very small amount of the first spice onto a paper plate. Then, take a little and try it! Do the same with all the spices.

Remember, you can't get faster at any skill or task until you're good at it first! With practice, speed will come.

BAKING

GET TO WORK!

The world is in love with food these days! Cookbooks are selling better than ever. TV is full of famous chefs, cooking races, game shows, and even kid chefs! But being a chef isn't about being famous. Being a chef is about always learning, tasting, experimenting, and inventing.

One thing is certain: As a chef, you'll never get bored. These days, we have more chances than ever to taste dishes from other countries! There's so much to learn, practice, and try—so get to work!

This recipe lets you experiment with ingredients! As you get to know spices and **herbs** better, this recipe will grow with you! Ask an adult to help you use the oven.

DINNER BREADSTICKS

YOU'LL NEED

a ball of pizza dough
(sold at many food stores)

oil/butter

spices/herbs

grated or finely shredded cheese

flour

oven

pastry/basting brush

baking sheet

soup bowl

DIRECTIONS

1. Preheat the oven using the directions on the dough.
2. Sprinkle flour onto a clean counter and your clean hands.
3. Roll an egg-sized ball of dough between your hands until it gets long and thin to form a breadstick.
4. Place it on a baking sheet.
5. Continue with the rest of the dough. If the dough gets sticky, add more flour to your hands and the counter.
6. Combine spices, herbs, and cheese in the bowl. Taste as you go!
7. Add melted butter/oil to the bowl and stir.
8. Use the brush to coat the breadsticks with the mixture.
9. Bake your breadsticks according to the dough's directions, watching them carefully.

21

GLOSSARY

butcher: someone who cuts and prepares meat for cooking. Or, to prepare meat for cooking.

caterer: someone whose business is providing food and drink when hired

cuisine: a style of cooking

flavor: the quality of something you can taste

fusion: food made by combining methods and ingredients from different areas of the world

herb: a plant or a part of a plant that is used to give flavor to food

ingredient: one of the things that is used to make a food

manage: to take care of and make decisions about things

menu: a list of foods that may be ordered. Or, the foods that will be served at a meal.

recipe: a set of instructions for making food

restaurant: a place where you can buy and eat a meal

specialize: to limit your work to one subject or thing to get really good at it

staff: a group of people who work for a business

FOR MORE INFORMATION

Books

Mahaney, Ian F. *Chef.* New York, NY: PowerKids Press, 2015.

Martin, Jacqueline Briggs. *Alice Waters and the Trip to Delicious.* Bellevue, WA: Readers to Eaters, 2014.

Siemens, Jared. *Chefs.* New York, NY: AV2 by Weigl, 2015.

Websites

Food Network
foodnetwork.com
This website for a TV channel devoted to food is filled with recipes, videos, and more!

Kid-Friendly Recipes
chef-in-training.com/2013/08/100-kid-friendly-recipes/
This blog lists over 100 recipes that kids can make!

Recipes for Kids
kidshealth.org/en/kids/recipes/#catrecipes
This website lists 63 recipes written just for kids to cook!

Publisher's note to educators and parents: Our editors have carefully reviewed these websites to ensure that they are suitable for students. Many websites change frequently, however, and we cannot guarantee that a site's future contents will continue to meet our high standards of quality and educational value. Be advised that students should be closely supervised whenever they access the Internet.

INDEX